PARAMAM

SAI VENKATESH

Contents

CHAPTER ONE

INTRODUCTION

It would be too naïve to assume that everything that is happening in the world is only happening at the physical, visible level alone. Even the most advanced scientist would admit that there is indeed a cosmic order, a force larger than individual entities, that operates and conducts everything in the universe – call it God, or nature, or destiny. Understanding this force and utilizing to one's benefit, in conjunction with the visible, physical aspects of life, is what gives a person completeness in life. This understanding and the mindset and lifestyle associated with it, is called Paramam.

However, there are two fundamental principles underlying the universe, that applies to everything contained within it – these are evolution and entropy. Indeed, even the acquisition of knowledge about this completeness also is subject to the same two principles.

Evolution is a principle of building up. Starting from the basic, most primitive, nature gently guides us towards higher and higher levels of living and abilities, until we reach the very zenith of our potentials. Think of the familiar evolution of life, from the smallest micro organisms all the way to us humans.

Entropy, on the contrary, is a principle of decay and disorder, which states that any entity in this universe will definitely experience an increase in disorder as time passes, so that it disintegrates and decays until it completely merges into its surroundings. Think of hot water being poured into a glass of cold water, and in due course it disintegrates and completely mixes to become a uniformly warm glass of water.

In terms of knowledge too, humanity has undergone a course of evolution, both on a personal and on a societal scale. On a personal scale, a human evolves and we get maturity physically, intellectually, emotionally and spiritually, as we age, and at the height of this, we become capable of understanding and accessing Paramam.

However, after a certain stage, typically at old age, a person is no longer at the zenith of his life. It is at that stage that, the person finds joy in disconnecting from society and culture, and retiring to the forests and mountains, living out his life until merging with nature, the very source and God he came from.

On a societal level, evolving from hunter gatherers and cavemen lifestyles, we have had centuries and millennia of culture and civilizational evolution, to bring us to this stage, where we have sufficient technology and globalization and other requirements needed to clearly access and understand Paramam.

Thus, we are as a society, at the height of maturity in all levels, so that we can understand and access Paramam. The outcome of that, is this very book, since this is that complete knowledge of Paramam.

Just as every mine needs a miner and discoverer to bring the treasures of the mine to the outside world, Paramam too needs an agent, to bring its knowledge outside to the world. This book being Paramam, the author is that agent.

Throughout history, the zenith and ultimate knowledge of Paramam being revealed one day, has been highly expected and awaited. This is why we find mentions of a future redeemer in every major culture and religion, be it Kalki of Hinduism, Messiah Second Coming of Judeo Christianity, Maitreya of Buddhism and so on, even including the immortal ruler of Nostradamus and Veera Bhoga Vasantha Raya of Kalajnanam – all these refer to the same person, the agent of the one ultimate Paramam.

To give people a context and cohesion and coherence to understanding it, religions also have built a past story, be it the Puranas, or Adamic Narratives, so that many prophets, many incarnations have been put forth, marking the stages of evolution, so that people can understand the lead up to this point in the universe, on both personal and societal levels.

This book, is intended to be used as the only and ultimate source of knowledge for completeness in life. It expounds not just a structure or an arrangement of divine powers, but also provides a language for communication with God, so that throughout life, by using this communication, lot of information can be exchanged with the divine powers, information itself being limitless by its very nature.

CHAPTER TWO

PARAMAM

What is Paramam? The word Paramam means the highest, most supreme entity that exists. What is the highest entity that can ever exist?

Now, we may say that God is the highest entity that exists, since God is controlling everything else. However, there is a reason to whatever God does, and that reason is to keep us happy and blissful, called Anandam. This means, that Anandam is higher than even God, and hence Paramam refers to that Anandam alone.

Through experience and self-inquiry, one can very easily find that the present world we live in and see around us in the wakeful state, is only as real as a world that we create for ourselves, within ourselves, as a dream every night. Thus, ultimately we the Self or Atma, are the creators of this world, and the energy of the Atma that creates and operates on this world, is God. This is why God always works situations in the world for the happiness of the Atma, since God is created for that very purpose. However, one finds this happiness without interruption only when one attains the state of evolutionary completeness, since, until this is attained, our mind may not align completely, and we may identify the desires of the mind falsely as the actual plans of the Atma.

Paramam is an arrangement of the divine forces that operate on the universe, in a 9x9 grid structure. The arrangement is directly aligned with the pattern of creation and space time itself, which is the fundamental seed of all creation. Thus, being aligned completely to the most fundamental energies of nature means that the access and control over nature, through God attains completeness here.

A glimpse of this fundamental creation process has been given in the book Aindiram, written by Mayan, in the ancient days long before the southern continent of Kumarikandam was submerged.

A dream, occurs inside us, much as a visualization of various ideas and thoughts in our mind, just as a storyline of thoughts is created as a movie. Thus, the basis for the present wake state world, which as hitherto explained, is also a dream, is also ideas and thoughts.

Thus, the creation process starts with a thought or idea in the mind, like an informational level blueprint for a house before the actual concrete house is built. This spark of creation as an idea or thought, is called Pranavam, and is symbolized by the sound Om.

The spark is just a single, small dot, called Moola Pulli, that throbs and vibrates radiantly with energy. The dot itself is square in shape, and quickly enough, manifests itself variegated as an 8x8 grid called Manduka Mandala – size-wise, it is still a dot, form-wise, that dot contains this 8x8 grid within itself. In that Mandala, those divine energies pertaining to exciting the thought alone are activated.

Now the thought spreads outwards. Every point in space and time in the entire universe contains the 8x8 Mandala, and a string connecting the central points of all the Mandalas in the whole universe, is called the Brahma Sutra. The energies active in the Mandala of every point determines the form or properties of matter or energy that exists in that point.

The 8x8 Mandala is called primal space, and the vibration of the Mandala due to certain elements of it being activated, creates time, since time is nothing but a marker that an entity has changed from one state to another, so that we can call one state as "before" and the other state as "after".

The vibration of specific points in the Mandala as mentioned above, creates an asymmetry, because of which the energy in the Mandala starts spinning one way or another. It is this spin that causes a curvature of the space itself around the Mandala, if seen in sufficient intensity, and this curvature is known as the force of gravity. The 8 fold aspect of the Mandala are nothing but the eight fundamental forces of subatomic particle physics, namely strong nuclear, electromagnetic, chirality, leptoquark stability, axionic matter preference, weak nuclear, mass field and particle familial generations.

However, the vibration or spin of the 8x8 Mandala causes instability and hence a modification in its state, and due to this, it assumes a form of 9x9, called Parama Sayika Mandala, also called Paramam. This modification occurs without any increase in mass or volume, and this state of 9x9, since it is after the spin has settled, is a state of stability and eternality.

Thus, Paramam has the best of both worlds, in that it has the estability and eternality of a final settled state, even while having the same mass and volume of the very initial state of creation. This is precisely the reason for the effectiveness of Paramam in bringing happiness to us in any situation, since it accesses both the initial and final instants of time simultaneously, forming a tunnel between the two as if they were stapled together, much like a wormhole. It is this power of Paramam that gives ultimate completeness in life, and hence was eagerly anticipated by all cultures and religions throughout history.

A key difference between the 8x8 and 9x9 is that, in the 8x8, the central element is a dot, at the junction of the four middle squares, and this means that the central element or focal point of the whole Mandala is at the thought level only. However, in the 9x9, the central element is a square, meaning that it is a visible and manifest form or location, accessible physically, and that forms the focal point of Paramam.

This location thus becomes the central point of not just earth, but the entire universe that has been created by the Atma. This is the location that has historically been called as Meru, Sumeru, Mahameru, Heaven, Paradise, Bindu and so on. This location geographically exists in present day Tamilnadu, India, on the outskirts of Ooty on the top of a hill called Tiger Hill Etha temple. Thus, this is the location that stores the energy and knowledge of Paramam in an unmanifest, subtle form, until we are evolutionarily ready to access this knowledge, at which point, we go there to obtain the energy. Even after obtaining this energy, a major feature of the life of completeness is frequent and periodical visits to Meru in counts of monthly intervals, in such a way that we get recharged time and time again from there. Ultimately, for a person who has indeed lived a Paramam life, when entropy sets in, he does retire and spend his life blissfully in Meru, detached from the world, until his very last breath. Indeed anybody who lives such a life of Paramam completely can be called the same Kalki or Messiah and so on.

The Peak of Meru

The path to the peak

While Paramam is indeed the ultimate structure and arrangement that offers us Anandam, the method of using the arrangement is equally important, and that is captured in two concepts, namely Thiru and Guru.

Thiru is the correct perception of God, which is as a loving, caring and gentle Mother, which is why we call it as Mother Nature. Just as a mother lovingly cares for her child, we view God as our own Mother, always connected to us, beside us as our sole eternal beloved relation, and her only focus and aim is entirely her child, meaning, our self and our happiness. Having this perception strongly ensures that we live life fully for love and happiness with her alone, and we seldom desire for anything else. It is only in the absence of any worldly desires in the mind that the mind is able to correctly reflect the true plans of the Atma, and one is able to understand the missions and tasks of one's own life. Further more, absence of desires removes distractions. This is because when we desire for something, usually some past failure that was caused by similar desire haunts us as fear, or some future anticipation of that desire makes us distracted, where we start building castles in the air. Absence of desires through love of Mother is the only solution for this.

The mother Amma certainly reciprocates our love, and gives us various situations through which she plays along with us and entertains us, her child, seated in her lap and fondled lovingly. The form of Mother in this loving, playful capacity is called Vaalai or Balaji, also called Venkatesha.

Guru means gravity, and is the correct mindset by which we increase the gravity of any creative thought or idea, so that it is carried out effectively and efficiently and realized physically to give us happiness eventually. Essentially, gravity is nothing but focus, since the more consistently and persistently we focus on a given thought, the more we create and reinforce it in the Manduka Mandala, and consequently, in the Paramam, and the more a single thought is reinforced in Paramam again and again, the more efficient it is realized physically. Thus, the correct mindset of Guru is essentially focusing on the present and giving complete commitment to the task that one undertakes with concurrence of Amma. Sraddha or Belief in the love of Amma, in that the result will definitely be happiness, creates a positive mindset that will reinforce the thought and increase gravity, while endurance of this Belief called Saburi, ensures that no matter what the difficulty of the task is, it will be carried out efficiently to success and happiness. Sraddha and Saburi together form the concept of Guru.

To represent this concept, historically Guru has been represented in many forms as various deities, saints and incarnations, starting with Dattatreya and ending with Sai.

In the forthcoming chapters, the forms of divine powers comprising Paramam will be explored. For convenience the 9x9 grid will be seen in 9 sections, each being a 3x3 grid. The names of the forms in each section will be outlined along with their functionality and powers, as well as remarks or additional names for each, as they have been known in different cultures and religions.

CHAPTER THREE

NORTHWEST

1. Annapoorni – Gives completion and strength. Also known as Visalakshi.

2. Raja Matangi – Gives correct understanding and perception, and ability to influence others with this perception. Also known as Shyamala, Meenakshi.

3. Nagakanni. Cultivates a competitive spirit, while ensuring our purity and victory. Also known as Manasa Devi, Nagapooshani, Kundalini, Sarpa, associated with Balarama, Sankarshana.

4. Rudra Chandi. Increases intensity of our creative thoughts to overpower adversities.

5. Asherah. Illuminates to take strides forward and progress. Chief Goddess of Judaism giving rise to the concept of Yahweh as consort.

6. Thara. Crosses over difficult situations and ensures our safety. Also called Ugra Tara or Nila Saraswati or Ekajati.

7. Lalitha. Gives playfulness and enjoyment in current situation. Also called Rajarajeshwari, Tripurasundari, Shodashi, Kamakshi.

8. Yakshini. Gives honour and reputation among people. Also called Kari Neeli, Pana Yakshi, Isakki, Yaaki.

9. Padmavathi. Blossoming of thoughts into favorable situations. Chief Goddess or Shasana Devata of Jainism, giving rise to concept of Tirthankaras such as Rishabhnath, Parshvanath and so on.

CHAPTER FOUR

NORTH

1. Radha Krishna. Enjoyment and exploring oneself through music and other pleasures.

2. Bhumi Devi. Gives fertility of new ideas , even while existing ones are physically realized. Also known as Prithvi, Vasundhara, Dharani.

3. Vayu. Gives speed and scattering of results. Also known as Prana Shakti.

4. Cernunnos. Enjoyment and ejaculatory bliss of orgasm. The God known originally as the phallic Pashupati and later as Nandi, as also the Wiccan Horned God, and also in Greek as Pan, and in later times, as Satan of Satanism.

5. Danu. Gives smoothness and free flow as well as rejuvenation. Also known as Kripi, Mother of Asuras.

6. Saraswati. Gives knowledge and wisdom. Also known as Sharada.

7. Kurukulla. Helps sail smoothly in turbulences. Also known as Mohini, Kurma, Dakini, Red Tara.

8. Yu Huang. Ruling over people and situations. God of Taoism as Jade Emperor, as the form of Daksha Prajapathi.

9. Miryam. Gives exaltation and elevation of status. Goddess of Christianity conceptualized as Jesus Christ.

CHAPTER FIVE

NORTHEAST

1. Kaali. Gives control and progress over time. Also known as Mahakali, Dakshinakali.

2. Yama. Gives restraint on adversities that violate our creative thoughts. Also known as Dharmaraja.

3. Nommo. Teachers of hidden details and wisdom from ancestral and extra terrestrial planes. God of alien planes from Sirius, as also the fish form Matsya.

4. Madhumathi. Gives sweetness and gentleness in life. Also called as Champakavalli in Siddha tradition, as well as Green Tara, conceptualizing Avalokiteshwara in Mahayana.

5. Somaskanda. Realizes creative thoughts into reality. Also known as Thyagaraja, Kameshwara, Ardhanarishwara.

6. Gitchi Manitou. Aligns thoughts with the spirit of surroundings and environment. Goddess originating the North American cultures.

7. Prathyangira. Reacts and responds to adversities severely. Also called Narasimhi.

8. Narayana. Gives elevation beyond human level and access to divine powers. Also called Mahavishnu, Vamana, Trivikrama.

9. Mielikki. Blesses with luck and good fortune. Uralic Goddess originating European cultures, also known as Bhagyalakshmi.

CHAPTER SIX

West

1. Vishwakarma. Operations and modifications on physical level. God of Freemasonry.

2. Kamadhenu. Yields desired fruits and results. Also called Surabhi or Nandini.

3. Garuda. Removes poisons and toxicity and gives strength. Also called Gandabherunda, Sharabheshwara and Akasha Bhairava.

4. Gayathri. Gives increased radiance and splendor. Also called Sandhya and Savitri.

5. Varuna. Gives excellence and control of wavy thoughts and mind. God of water and the oceans.

6. Allat. Blesses with prosperity and harvest of results. Goddess originating Islam as Allah.

7. Veerabhadra. Gives courage and auspiciousness. Also called Manibhadra and Aghora.

8. Ganesha. Gives transcendence over classifications and barriers. Also called vancha Kalpalatha and Vinayaki.

9. Kubera. Gives abundance and fame. Also called Vaishravana and Yaksharaja.

CHAPTER SEVEN

CENTER

1. Guhyeshwari. Hides important information from wrong hands. Also called Guhya Kali and Kalasankarshini.

2. Karuppaswami. Punishes violators of righteousness and truth. Also called Veeran, Madaswamy, Sudalaimadan,

Munishwaran.

3. Mahalakshmi. Blesses with abundance and wealth. Also called Sridevi.

4. Bhuvaneshwari. Controls and channels energies cosmically.

5. Valli. Gives rejuvenated strength and positivity. Also called Kathayi, Katyayani, Kaumari and Goddess central to Meru.

6. Durga. Breaks barriers and fortresses thus enabling progress. Also called Vaishno Devi.

7. Chamunda. Stops and punishes evil adversities from astral and dead soul levels. Also known as Pishachini, Soshini, Raktakali.

8. Brahma. Gives expansion and exploration of ideas in all directions.

9. Baalaa. Gives vigor and lively energy of youthfulness. Also known as Ashoka Sundari and Kanyakumari, of the submerged continent. Represents Venkatesh in Paramam.

CHAPTER EIGHT

East

1. Indra. Gives power over senses and organs Indriya, increasing sensitivity. Also called Sampatkari, Airavateshwari.

2. Rakshasa. Gives protection from adversities. Also known as Brahma Rakshasa, Kadawara.

3. Umay. Gives affection and love towards children. Known as Uma, originator of Shamanist traditions centered on Siberia.

4. Varahi. Gives excellence of work and activity. Known as Dandanatha.

5. Shiva. Gives welfare and auspiciousness. Also known as Nataraja, Kalyana sundareshwara, Bholenath.

6. Amaterasu. Gives illumination of things and methods. Goddess of Shinto religion originating Asian cultures.

7. Manonmani. Gives presence of mind and stability of emotions. Goddess of Siddhas, also known as Siddhilakshmi, Kamalamba.

8. Aditi. Expansion and conceiving even the infinite without limitations. Also known as Bahuchara and Lajja Gauri.

9. Ousire. Knowledge and information from the dead souls, called Pithrus and Prethas. Egyptian God originating African cultures.

CHAPTER NINE

SOUTHWEST

1. Hanuman. Gives strength and clever mind. Also called Anjaneya and Kesari and Atharvani

2. Subrahmanya. Gives positivity and confidence to handle anything easily. Also called Karthikeya, Muruga, Sharavanabhava.

3. Rama. Gives enjoyment in present situations , no matter what difficulties are around. Represents Sai in the Paramam.

4. Vanashankari. Gives good and beneficial results. Goddess of forest known as Vana Devatha, Shakambari, Shatodari.

5. Vishnumaya. Gives pervasiveness and spreading of our creative strengths. Known as Chathan, Muthappan.

6. Kannaki. Gives auspiciousness and extreme purity. Known as Bhadrakali, Subhadra, Sarvamangala.

7. Kethu. Gives control of reptilian brain, impulsive instincts. Denotes comets and descending lunar node.

8. Raahu. Gives increases of enjoyment and attraction and appeal. Denotes eclipses and ascending lunar node.

9. Shani. Slows down superficial tendencies and gives depth and focus. Saturn.

CHAPTER TEN

SOUTH

1. Shitala. Gives cooling down and settling of things. Also known as Jwarahara.

2. Rathi. Gives pleasure of arousal and stimulation. Also associated with Manmatha, Apsara of Thai-Khmer culture.

3. Sastha. Gives ruling and command over situations and things. Also known as Ayyappa, Dharmasastha, Manikanta.

4. Bagalamukhi. Restrains speech and power of adversities. Also known as Pachi, Mookambika, Nakuleshwari.

5. Bhairava. Causes fear among adversities. God of dead spirits called Vethalas and Bhoothas.

6. Jyeshta. Gives access to most primordial level of creation and hence highest level of power. Also known as Nirruthi, Dhumavathi, with daughter Pralayambika and son Maandhi Kapalishwara.

7. Shukra. Gives knowledge of how to benefit oneself in any situation. Venus.

8. Brihaspathi. Gives knowledge and wisdom of how to expand oneself. Jupiter.

9. Budha. Gives sharpness and clarity of intellect. Mercury.

CHAPTER ELEVEN

SOUTHEAST

1. Renuka. Goddess of finalizing and establishing creation fulfilling our wishes. Also known as Chhinnamasta, Vajrayogini, Mariamman, Angalamman, Ellaiamman and associated with Parashurama.

2. Tiraskarini. Creates situations for revealing and exposing new information. Also known as Ashwarudha.

3. Ixchel. Gives healing and medicinal powers. Mayan Goddess of central and south American cultures.

4. Agni. Gives fierceness and ability to dissolve anything into ourselves. God originating Zoroastrianism as Ahura Mazda. Also conceptualized as Draupadi.

5. Mahamaya. Exposes hidden information by revealing the hidden screen. Goddess originating Buddha and Buddhism.

6. Altjira. Accesses and operates on the level of astral and visualizations to establish our creative ideas which then reflect physically. God of Australian and Oceania cultures.

7. Mangala. Gives auspiciousness and conclusions. Mars.

8. Chandra. Gives calmness and serenity. Moon

9. Surya. Gives brightness and knowledge of things sustaining life. Sun.

CHAPTER TWELVE

CONCLUSION

The Paramam as an arrangement of divine forces have been explained. By having these forms in a randomized item or image generator, one can use this as a system called Prashnam to ask questions from God. Here, one asks the concerned question, and the form among all 81 that pops up in a random image selector holds the answer to the question asked. In case of a binary yes/no type of question such as confirming interpretation to the received answer of a previous question, one can use feminine deities as a yes and masculine deities as a no answer.

Thus, this forms a communication method where one can be in touch with the divine, asking the big questions, but also the most mundane and silliest of questions, all the while spending time with Amma in happy love. There is no end and limit for such knowledge gained through these conversations of love. The very act of asking and obtaining a form as an answer triggers that very form in the creation space, and further consequently in the world as well.

In Paramam, as a general rule, we assume that gravity acts from top to down and left to right. Furthermore, we can also explore the arrangement and the path between two given forms in the Paramam Yantra, using moves from one to another very similar to the chess game.

9 798887 330631

Printed by Libri Plureos GmbH in Hamburg,
Germany